C000215816

To Mighty Thea,

Welcome to the world!

I imagine you becoming such a creatively strong force for good Thea! You're such a beautiful gift... Here's a little gift as we celebrate you!

Huge love, Andy, Rho, Noah + Anna
x

JANE AUSTEN

Frances Lincoln Limited
74–77 White Lion Street
London N1 9PF
www.franceslincoln.com

A catalogue record for this book is available
from the British Library.

ISBN 978-0-7112-3666-0

1 2 3 4 5 6 7 8 9

FRANCES LINCOLN LIMITED
PUBLISHERS

JANE AUSTEN

by Zena Alkayat and Nina Cosford

'Which of all my important nothings
shall I tell you first?'

Letter, 1808

JANE AUSTEN WAS BORN ON 16th DECEMBER 1775 IN STEVENTON, HAMPSHIRE. SHE LIVED IN THE VILLAGE RECTORY WITH HER FATHER GEORGE AND MOTHER CASSANDRA.

THE RECTORY WAS ALSO A WORKING FARM, COMPLETE WITH COWS, CHICKENS AND DUCKS, AS WELL AS WHEAT, BARLEY AND HOPS. JANE GREW UP WITH SIX BROTHERS AND ONE SISTER.

The Austen

Rev George Austen

James
Austen

George
Austen

Edward
Austen

Henry
Austen

Family Tree

Cassandra Leigh

Cassandra
Austen

Francis 'Frank'
Austen

Jane
Austen

Charles
Austen

JANE'S FATHER WAS A PARSON AND A FARMER, BUT TO SUPPLEMENT HIS FAMILY'S INCOME, HE AND MRS AUSTEN TURNED THE RECTORY INTO A SMALL BOYS' BOARDING SCHOOL.

SO JANE WAS USED TO
BEING AROUND MALE COMPANY —
AND LOTS AND LOTS OF BOOKS.

AS YOUNG CHILDREN, JANE AND CASSANDRA WERE INSEPARABLE. THE SISTERS WENT TO BOARDING SCHOOL TOGETHER WHERE THEY LEARNED SPELLING, FRENCH, MATHS, NEEDLEWORK AND DANCE.

WHEN JANE WAS 11, HER COUSIN
ELIZA CAME TO SPEND CHRISTMAS AT
STEVENTON. ELIZA WAS MYSTERIOUS
AND STRIKING, AND HER LIFE WAS AS
FANTASTICAL AS FICTION. SHE WAS
MARRIED TO A EUROPEAN COUNT,
SPOKE FLUENT FRENCH AND WORE
CONTINENTAL FASHIONS.

HER GLAMOUR CAUSED A STIR: THE
AUSTEN BOYS FLIRTED AND JANE
FOUND A LIFELONG FRIEND.

Eliza

THE AUSTENS LOVED TO
PUT ON PLAYS.

THEY INVITED FRIENDS TO TAKE ON
ROLES AND PAINTED SETS AND PROPS
FOR THEIR PRODUCTIONS.

SCENE ONE

THEY ALSO LOVED TO WRITE.
JANE'S MOTHER WROTE VERSE,
AND HER BROTHER JAMES WAS
A SKILLED POET. JANE PREFERRED
PROSE, AND FILLED NOTEBOOKS
WITH WILD AND WITTY STORIES.

ALL AROUND HER, PEOPLE WERE
GETTING MARRIED. AND THE SUBJECT
OF MONEY WAS NEVER FAR AWAY.

JANE HEARD HOW COUSIN ELIZA
WAS BORN IN INDIA AFTER HER
MOTHER WENT THERE DETERMINED
TO FIND A HUSBAND AMONG
THE ENGLISH TRADERS.

CASSANDRA WAS SOON ENGAGED
TO A YOUNG CLERGYMAN NAMED
THOMAS FOWLE. BUT NEITHER
HAD ANY MONEY, AND A MARRIAGE
WAS UNLIKELY TO BE ARRANGED
WITHOUT IT.

BY HER LATE TEENS, JANE HAD
BEGUN WORK ON A NOVELLA.

'LADY SUSAN' WAS ABOUT A
SCHEMING WOMAN ON THE
HUNT FOR TWO HUSBANDS, ONE
FOR HERSELF, ANOTHER FOR
HER DAUGHTER.

IT DIDN'T TAKE LONG FOR
JANE'S FAMILY TO RECOGNISE
HER EXTRAORDINARY TALENT.
HER FATHER WAS EXCEPTIONALLY
PROUD, AND BOUGHT HER A SMALL
MAHOGANY WRITING TABLE FOR
HER 19th BIRTHDAY.

JANE LOVED TO DANCE AND
ATTENDED BALLS HOSTED BY
THE GENTRY IN THE VILLAGE.

THE FURNITURE WOULD BE PUSHED
BACK, A NEIGHBOUR MIGHT PICK
UP HIS FIDDLE, AND SOMEONE
WOULD PLAY THE PIANO.

'To be fond of dancing was a certain step towards falling in love.'

'Pride and Prejudice', 1813

JANE HAD A GIFT FOR SOCIAL
OBSERVATION, AND A SHARP EYE
FOR HUMAN FOLLY. NOT YET 20,
SHE BEGAN WRITING HER FIRST
NOVEL 'ELINOR AND MARIANNE',
WHICH WENT ON TO BECOME
'SENSE AND SENSIBILITY'.

MEANWHILE THE BATTLES OF
THE FRENCH REVOLUTION WERE
BEING WAGED. ENGLISH CAVALRYMEN
WERE NEEDED AND FOUR OF JANE'S
BROTHERS WERE INVOLVED IN THE
MILITARY AND THE NAVY.

COUSIN ELIZA'S HUSBAND WAS KILLED IN FRANCE, LEAVING HER WIDOWED WITH A SMALL CHILD.

APART FROM A GROWING NUMBER
OF OFFICERS AROUND TOWN,
LIFE IN STEVENTON REMAINED
UNCHANGED. JANE CONTINUED TO
FLIRT AND DANCE WITH ELIGIBLE
YOUNG MEN - AND THEN SHE MET
LAW STUDENT TOM LEFROY.

Tom

THEIR ATTRACTION TO EACH
OTHER WAS OBVIOUS TO THE
NEIGHBOURS AND, DESPITE ONLY
KNOWING HIM A SHORT TIME, JANE
WAS NOT SHY IN PROCLAIMING HER
INTEREST IN TOM.

'I am almost afraid to tell you
how my Irish friend and I behaved.
Imagine to yourself everything most
profligate and shocking in the way of
dancing and sitting down together.'

Letter, January 1796

TOM WAS UNDER PRESSURE TO DO WELL IN HIS CAREER AND MARRY ADVANTAGEOUSLY. AND JANE WAS A GIRL WITH NO FORTUNE. AS QUICKLY AS SHE HAD FALLEN FOR HIM, HE DISAPPEARED FROM HER LIFE.

JANE CONTINUED TO WORK STEADILY. BY OCTOBER 1796 SHE HAD BEGUN WRITING 'FIRST IMPRESSIONS', WHICH WOULD GO ON TO BECOME 'PRIDE AND PREJUDICE'. SHE FINISHED THE MANUSCRIPT IN LESS THAN A YEAR AND RETURNED TO 'SENSE AND SENSIBILITY' TO RESTRUCTURE AND REVISE IT.

SHE WOULD READ HER WORK
ALOUD TO HER FAMILY.

Jane's

Quill

wax & seal

Cassandra's letters

penknife

ink

father's portrait

clock

scissors

Desk

small mirror

lavender

string

spectacles

candlestick

manuscripts

first editions

'SENSE AND SENSIBILITY' WAS ABOUT SISTERS ELINOR AND MARIANNE (ONE DISCREET AND WELL BEHAVED, THE OTHER OPEN AND RECKLESS IN LOVE), AS WELL AS MERCENARY MARRIAGES, CLASS, MONEY, MANIPULATION AND MANNERS.

Darcy

'PRIDE AND PREJUDICE' FOLLOWS THE HIGHS AND LOWS OF FIVE BENNET SISTERS, INCLUDING ELIZABETH BENNET WHO HAS A TURBULENT RELATIONSHIP WITH THE HAUGHTY AND HANDSOME MR DARCY.

MR AUSTEN WAS SO PLEASED
WITH HIS DAUGHTER'S MANUSCRIPTS
THAT HE SENT 'PRIDE AND
PREJUDICE' TO LONDON PUBLISHER
THOMAS CADELL IN 1797. HE VERY
SWIFTLY RECEIVED AN ANSWER.

Declined
by return of
post

MORE BAD NEWS WAS TO FOLLOW.
TO MAKE MONEY FOR HIS FUTURE,
CASSANDRA'S BETROTHED HAD
BECOME A CHAPLAIN TO AN ENGLISH
REGIMENT IN THE WEST INDIES. BUT
HE DIED OF YELLOW FEVER BEFORE
HE COULD MAKE HIS FORTUNE.

CASSANDRA RECEIVED £1000
IN HIS WILL.

DEVASTATED BY HER LOST LOVE,
SHE NEVER MARRIED.

JANE'S BROTHER HENRY, HOWEVER, WAS BUSY COURTING THE STILL EXOTIC COUSIN ELIZA, AND SUCCEEDED IN WINNING HER HAND.

ELIZA - TEN YEARS HIS SENIOR - ENJOYED THE SOCIAL SCENE AND COULD BE SPOTTED CARRYING HER PUG AROUND LONDON.

ALL AROUND JANE, SMALL
FISSURES WERE APPEARING IN THE
ESTABLISHED SOCIAL STRUCTURE.
MARY WOLLSTONECRAFT'S
'VINDICATION OF THE RIGHTS OF
WOMAN' (PUBLISHED IN 1792) WAS
A CONTROVERSIAL INDICTMENT OF
SEXUAL INEQUALITY.

AND JANE WAS A KEEN FAN
OF MORALIST SAMUEL JOHNSON,
WHOSE ESSAYS SUPPORTED SERVICE
TO ONE'S FELLOW MAN AND
DILIGENCE (NOT INHERITANCE) AS
A PATH TO PROSPERITY.

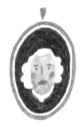

AS HER BROTHERS MARRIED AND HAD CHILDREN, JANE FELT THE PRESSURE OF AWKWARD MATCHMAKING. SHE ALSO HAD THE CHANCE TO OBSERVE FAMILY LIFE WHILE VISITING HER BROTHERS AND HELPING WITH HER MANY NIECES AND NEPHEWS.

JANE BEGAN WORK ON 'SUSAN' (LATER KNOWN AS 'NORTHANGER ABBEY'). THE ACTION WAS SET IN THE FASHIONABLE RESORT TOWN OF BATH, AND IN 1799 JANE HAD THE CHANCE TO TAKE A TRIP WITH HER MOTHER.

WHENEVER SHE AND CASSANDRA
WERE APART, JANE WROTE REAMS
AND REAMS, FILLING HER SISTER IN
ON DAILY EVENTS.

BUT CASSANDRA DESTROYED
MANY OF JANE'S LETTERS,
ENSURING HER SISTER'S CAUSTIC
JOKES AND CONFIDENTIAL
THOUGHTS REMAINED PRIVATE.

AT THE TURN OF THE CENTURY,
JANE'S PARENTS (NOW IN THEIR
OLD AGE) DECIDED QUITE SUDDENLY
TO LEAVE BEHIND THE RECTORY'S
FARM LIFE IN FAVOUR OF THE
PLEASURES OF BATH.

HUNDREDS OF BOOKS WERE SOLD
AND THE HOUSE WAS PACKED UP.

BATH WAS DESIGNED FOR SOCIALISING. THERE WERE THEATRE SHOWS AND DANCES, REJUVENATING WATERS TO SOAK IN, SHOPS TO VISIT AND PARADING GENTRY TO ADMIRE.

PEOPLE-WATCHING WAS ONE OF
BATH'S CHIEF ATTRACTIONS.

Bath

THE AUSTENS MOVED INTO
4 SYDNEY PLACE, A TERRACED
HOUSE OVERLOOKING PRETTY
GARDENS. DESPITE ITS APPEAL, JANE
WASN'T CONTENT WITH HER NEW
LIFE. IT TOOK HER SEVERAL YEARS
TO RETURN TO HER MANUSCRIPTS.

JANE TRIED TO MAKE THE BEST
OF HER NEW SURROUNDINGS.
SHE EXPLORED THE SOUTH WEST
COAST, TRAVELLING TO DAWLISH,
TEIGNMOUTH AND LYME REGIS. SHE
RAMBLED ALONG THE CLIFFS AND
TOOK DIPS IN THE SEA WITH
A BATHING MACHINE.

Lyme Regis

ON ONE TRIP, JANE VISITED HER
FRIENDS ALETHEA AND CATHERINE
BIGG IN HAMPSHIRE, AND SPENT
TIME WITH THEIR BROTHER HARRIS.

HARRIS WAS AN AWKWARD YOUNG
MAN WITH A STAMMER. HE WAS
ALSO HEIR TO A SMALL FORTUNE.

ON 2nd DECEMBER 1802,
HARRIS PROPOSED TO JANE.
AND SHE ACCEPTED.

WHEN SHE WOKE THE NEXT DAY,
SHE SOUGHT OUT HARRIS AND
POLITELY EXPLAINED SHE WASN'T
WILLING TO MARRY HIM.

HE FOUND A WIFE TWO YEARS LATER.
SHE BORE HIM TEN CHILDREN.

IN 1803, JANE'S BROTHER HENRY
SENT 'NORTHANGER ABBEY' TO
LONDON PUBLISHER RICHARD CROSBY,
WHO AGREED TO A FEE OF £10 FOR
THE BOOK - BUT THEN FAILED
TO PUBLISH IT.

JANE'S SLOWLY RETURNING
ENTHUSIASM FOR WRITING
STALLED AGAIN WHEN HER FATHER
WAS TAKEN ILL AND DIED IN 1805.
HIS DEATH HAD A HUGE IMPACT ON
HIS DEPENDENTS JANE, CASSANDRA
AND THEIR MOTHER.

THEY WERE COMPELLED TO TAKE
A HOUSE IN SOUTHAMPTON WITH
JANE'S BROTHER FRANK.

LIFE SOON SETTLED DOWN.
JANE'S BROTHER EDWARD OFFERED
HIS MOTHER AND SISTERS A COTTAGE
IN CHAWTON, HAMPSHIRE.

IT HAD SIX BEDROOMS AND A
KITCHEN GARDEN. THE AUSTEN
WOMEN MOVED THERE IN THE
SUMMER OF 1809.

Chawton

LIFE AT CHAWTON WAS PEACEFUL.
JANE'S MOTHER (NOW IN HER
SEVENTIES) WOULD SPEND HER DAYS
PLANTING POTATOES AND TENDING
TO THE FLOWER BEDS.

AND JANE WOULD TAKE WALKS
TO NEARBY ALTON, WHERE SHE
WOULD GO SHOPPING WITH HER
SISTER AND POST HER LETTERS.

AT CHAWTON JANE FOUND THE
CHANCE TO WORK AGAIN. SHE
TIDIED UP 'SENSE AND SENSIBILITY',
AND HENRY FOUND A PUBLISHER
WILLING TO PRINT THE BOOK AT
THE AUTHOR'S EXPENSE. HENRY AND
ELIZA PAID THE COSTS.

THE BOOK SOLD OUT OF ITS
FIRST PRINT RUN PRICED AT
15 SHILLINGS. JANE EARNED £140
IN ROYALTIES IN TWO YEARS.

OVER THE NEXT FEW YEARS, JANE MADE SEVERAL VISITS TO HER BROTHER HENRY AND WIFE ELIZA'S HOUSE IN SLOANE STREET IN LONDON. SHE TOOK WALKS TO THE CENTRE OF TOWN AND CARRIAGE RIDES TO THE THEATRE.

London

JANE PUBLISHED ANONYMOUSLY, AND
HER LIFE AT CHAWTON CONTINUED
UNDISTURBED. HER DAILY DUTY WAS
TO MAKE A BREAKFAST OF TEA AND
TOAST ON THE FIRE. SHE WOULD
WAKE UP EARLY AND PRACTISE AT
THE PIANO BEFORE THE REST OF
THE HOUSEHOLD STIRRED.

Georgian

cream
jug

shell
dish

silver cutlery

china
plate

slice

pickle

fruit bowl

Dining

sauce boat

mustard
pot

silver
mug

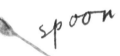

spoon

sweetmeats

candelabra

teacup

teapot

IN 1811, SHE BEGAN WORK ON 'MANSFIELD PARK'. THE NOVEL CENTRED AROUND FANNY PRICE, A YOUNG LADY WITH HIGH MORALS AND NO INCOME. THRUST INTO THE UPPER ECHELONS OF SOCIETY, FANNY REMAINS STOIC IN THE FACE OF FRIVOLITY AND TEMPTATION.

BUOYED BY THE CRITICAL SUCCESS OF 'SENSE AND SENSIBILITY' AND ITS POPULARITY AMONG THE RICH AND FASHIONABLE, JANE OFFERED THE SAME PUBLISHER (THOMAS EGERTON OF THE MILITARY LIBRARY) THE COPYRIGHT TO 'PRIDE AND PREJUDICE' IN 1812.

THE BOOK SOLD TO THE PUBLIC FOR
18 SHILLINGS. SHE RECEIVED £110.

READERS FELL IN LOVE WITH
ELIZABETH BENNET. AND JANE WAS
PARTIAL TO THE CHARACTER TOO.

'I must confess that I think her
as delightful a creature as ever
appeared in print, how I shall be able to
tolerate those who do not like her
at least, I do not know.'

Letter, January 1813

ELIZABETH

JANE MOVED SWIFTLY ON TO HER
NEXT HEROINE, STARTING 'EMMA'
IN EARLY 1814 AND FINISHING THE
NOVEL IN SPRING 1815, JUST AS
'MANSFIELD PARK' WAS PUBLISHED.

'EMMA' WAS A COMEDY OF
ERRORS REVOLVING AROUND
ILL-ADVISED MATCHMAKING AND
MISGUIDED MANIPULATION.

JANE'S IDENTITY AS AN AUTHOR
WAS GRADUALLY REVEALED, AND THE
PRINCE REGENT DECLARED HIMSELF
A FAN. HE MADE IT KNOWN THAT
HE WANTED JANE TO DEDICATE
'EMMA' TO HIM.

AS JANE TURNED 40 IN DECEMBER 1815, 2,000 COPIES OF 'EMMA' WERE PRINTED (COMPLETE WITH A DEDICATION TO THE ROYAL ADMIRER). THE BOOK SOLD FOR 21 SHILLINGS.

To his
Royal Highness
the Prince Regent,
this work is, by his
royal highness's
permission, most
respectfully
dedicated

AFTER THIS FLURRY OF PUBLISHING
TRIUMPHS, CRITICAL SUCCESS
AND MODEST FAME, JANE BEGAN
TO FEEL UNWELL. SHE KEPT BUSY
WRITING 'THE ELLIOTS', WHICH
WENT ON TO BECOME 'PERSUASION'.
BUT IT WOULD BE PUBLISHED
POSTHUMOUSLY.

'PERSUASION' WAS AS CLOSELY OBSERVED AS JANE'S PREVIOUS NOVELS. HEROINE ANNE ELLIOT WAS A YOUNG WOMAN TALKED OUT OF MARRYING A MAN DEEMED TOO LOWLY FOR HER, ONLY TO MEET HIM SOME TEN YEARS LATER AS A RICH, SUCCESSFUL AND ADMIRED NAVY CAPTAIN.

DESPITE HER REFUSAL TO ADMIT SERIOUS ILLNESS, JANE WAS SOON CONFINED TO HER BED. IN APRIL 1817 SHE PRIVATELY WROTE HER WILL, AND SOON AFTER WAS TAKEN TO LODGINGS AT 8 COLLEGE STREET IN WINCHESTER TO BE NEAR HER SURGEON.

'If I live to be an old woman I must expect to wish I had died now, blessed in the tenderness of such a family, before I survived either them or their affection.'

Letter, May 1817

ON 18th JULY 1817, JANE
DIED PEACEFULLY WITH HER HEAD
RESTING ON HER SISTER'S LAP.
SHE WAS 41.

'She was the sun of my life,
the gilder of every pleasure,
the soother of every sorrow.'

Cassandra Austen, july 1817

Acknowledgements

The author gratefully acknowledges the information and inspiration provided by Claire Tomalin's wonderful biography *Jane Austen: A Life*. Further thanks go to Joan Strasbaugh, author of *The List Lover's Guide to Jane Austen*, for her consultation on the book. Her expertise was invaluable.

The illustrator would like to extend her love and thanks to Ali, Ma, Pops, Jojo and Chester.

The quotations used in this publication have been sourced from the following:

Jane Austen's Letters, ed Deirdre Le Faye (Oxford University Press).

Selected Letters, ed Vivien Jones, (Oxford University Press).

Pride and Prejudice, Jane Austen (Penguin).